Darkness to Empowerment

DARKNESS TO EMPOWERMENT

FINDING YOURSELF AGAIN
AFTER SEXUAL ABUSE

MANDY EMMINS

Cover design and typeset by BookPOD

ISBN: 978-1-7645693-0-9 (pbk) eISBN: 978-1-7645693-1-6(ebook)

A catalogue record for this book is available from the National Library of Australia

*This book is dedicated to my husband, who passed away
suddenly and unexpectedly just as I was putting the
finishing touches to this 7 years in the making book.*

*He was my soul mate and life partner and
my biggest supporter and cheer squad.*

*He was there for me on every step of my
journey and never once doubted me.*

*He believed me and loved me unconditionally, from the
first moment we met until we said our last goodbye.*

*So, Steve this is for you, I will love
you "til the stars don't shine"*

Contents

Finding Your Power and Truth Once Again

I am NOT a Medical Professional.

*I am a Qualified Holistic Counsellor
and Women's wellbeing coach.*

A Psychic Clairvoyant and Universal Energy Healer.

A sexual abuse survivor.

*Someone who has walked the path from darkness
to find MY own Empowerment within.*

If I was to write a book on empowerment, where should I start.? Should I start at the point I found this elusive empowerment or the moment / moments that led to my not feeling empowered?

That is the question, right? because when you picked up this book that is what you wanted to know.

I disagree you picked up this book for various reasons, someone recommended it, you saw it advertised somewhere, you liked the title, or it simply resonated with you in some way. Because the truth is, we are all looking for empowerment in some ways in our life. From freeing ourselves from domestic drudgery, or bad career choices or violence or abuse or a many numbers of reasons you now feel disempowered – whatever the reason you picked up this book right here and right now doesn't really matter. All that matters is you now have it and all I can hope to achieve is to help you find some small peace of mind, some small bit within you that stands up and is recognised and accounted for who you truly are, a unique one of a kind, no one ever was or ever will be made just like you again. That is EMPOWERMENT, that is your power – knowing who you are and standing in your truth. For some it can take years to sort this out and become comfortable in your own skin, others move into it early in their life. We can only hope to raise young girls who find their power sooner in life than we have or did.

That darkness that is living without power is a fully encompassing thing, for some it comes in an instant, for some it takes a few years to realise you lost it or if you ever really had it. You lost that connection within yourself to say HEY this is NOT OK. If you are feeling wrong about something being done or said to you and you do nothing for whatever reasons that takes away a piece of your power. NOW I totally understand because I have been there, there are times when for your own health and safety it is better to say and do nothing and let the moment slide on by.

My point in writing this book is, it's about taking back YOUR power, empowering YOU to do and say and live the life you genuinely want. Why do we follow others so blindly thinking their lives look so amazing, that we want that as well! We idolise sports people and actors, WHY do we not idolise ourselves. WHY do we not build ourselves up. We are just as worthy, and just as impressive as they are with their million-dollar PR campaigns telling us all exactly how fabulous they are. It Is all smoke and mirrors and we soon learn that for ourselves. As no one can pretend to be something they are not forever, and they inevitably fall over. We learn that their lives are just as messed up as ours. Look at Elvis, Michael Jackson, Amy Winehouse, Whitney Houston etc – the list goes on and on. A fake life is a harder thing to keep going than living an honest and true self life.

So, let's stop faking it, lets stop pretending, lets get real and be real and acknowledge once and for all...we are NOT perfect but then neither is anyone else and that is 100% OK... So, follow me now on this journey from darkness to empowerment. Let me help you to see yourself as the truly incredible and unique person you are and love yourself for who you are. Can you look at yourself in the mirror and tell yourself you love you? Or even I like you.?

That is a true test, and one thing that personally took me years to do.

There is no judgement in this book, there is no quick fix and there is no magic pill that will take away your pain – sorry.

I am nothing if not honest and to be honest I can be blunt. However I come from a place of love, I want you to be your very best person possible – however that looks to you.

Let's get going, let's move forward and embrace your empowerment.

The only thing to fear, is fear itself

– Franklin. D Roosevelt.

The only thing to fear, is fear itself

- Franklin. D Roosevelt.

The Darkness

This book is about moving forward after sexual abuse. It will give you the tools to help you do this. It will show you there is life after abuse. There is light at the end. I promise you.

There are mental health issues that will require a medical diagnosis and medical intervention where needed.

There are also plenty of avenues to gain help, from phone lines, to online forums, to support groups, so reach out because there are people who know how you feel and there are people who can help.

When I talk about The Darkness it is not as some dark evil thing that invades us. It is that veil like moment when night-time starts to change from daytime, where darkness descends on us, and we cannot see the way forward clearly or ahead or any hope in our future.

Where you feel that the darkness of the night never leaves you – even in the bright fullness of daylight hours.

It can be a heaviness that envelopes us, we just feel trapped within our own mind space and our own thoughts. Nothing anyone else says or does - or we read or do can bring us out of this darkness until we are ready to lift this veil again ourselves.

People with medically diagnosed Depression refer to it as the Black dog descending. It is depressive and oppressive and can be hard to explain to others. That feeling of not wanting to get out of bed. It is not laziness it is simply we cannot face things; we cannot deal with anything; we want the safety and security of the doona over our heads and to stay there for as long as we need.

That feeling of complete mental and physical exhaustion. We think no one else knows what this feels like, we think we are all alone, we believe no one would believe us anyway so why tell our story, we may feel ashamed as if we somehow did something wrong to bring this all down upon ourselves. You may feel unworthy of help. You may not want to ask others for help. You might feel like no one would understand how you are feeling anyway so why bother.

I can assure you NONE of that is true. When you do start to reach out to others, you will find, sadly way too many others who have experienced the same things as you, who have undergone worse than you could possibly have imagined. Yet appear in life to have it all together or simply disappear into their own heads and space. They retreat or become reclusive.

During my research for this book, I spoke with women with various stories of abuse, trauma and recovery.

- Repeatedly being raped by a family member from 2 years old to 13. As a young child she knew no different, she was told this was how he was showing her love and affection. That he loved her so much. It wasn't until later in life this women remembered and realised, she has been abused, not loved.

- Being abused and raped by a family friend, who used a bottle or screwdriver handle to rape, so he left no trace of semen. This was a trusted family friend, the girls parents left her and her sister with this man to baby sit them, whilst they went out. The girls tried telling their parents but were not believed. Even after they had told their parents, their parent still left them with this man several more times.

Even when she eventually went to the police and a court case was pending – her parents still believed her abuser – NOT their own daughters.

- An Uncle who molested three of his own nieces without either of them being aware of each other's abuse, thinking they were alone until later in life when they discovered each other's truth.

- A girl who was molested by two childhood friends in a public swimming pool. To anyone looking on it appeared they were play fighting and mucking around. The girl was left traumatised and verbally threatened to keep quiet by these two boys she thought were friends.

- A church leader who repeatedly abused both boys and girls over years, none knew of the others being abused until later in life. One victim didn't realise the depth of this perpetrators abuse until he saw a TV program about this church elder, once other victims decided to take legal action. There are now hundred of victims who have come forward, there could be hundred more that have not. It is also now known that several of this person victims committed suicide.

- Or the women who was repeatedly abused by her husband, the father of her two children, over many years. She hid this all from her family and friends. Blaming marks on her skin and bruises as other things, accidents, bumps etc. Until finally she had enough once her children became old enough to ask questions and see the truth. This gave her the courage to move out and start moving forward in her life.

Sadly, these are just a few stories, there are far too many more to mention here. The statistics on historic child abuse are staggering. There are actually more people who have been abused than have not in the 50- to 60-year-old age group. Stats available from www.bravehearts.org.au show that sexual assault cases have increased since 1993 from 69 to 121 victims per 100,000 in 2021. My thoughts are these stats reflect the fact that more people are feeling empowered enough to report their abuse than in previous years where we kept quiet.

However the shocking fact is that sexual abuse is not going away. Whilst the struggle to change society and the feeling around abuse is a HUGE one, it is not something I will raise in this book.

I am writing this to help people overcome sexual abuse, my feelings are that as we continue to empower ourselves we will help to overcome issues around society and sexual abuse. Sadly the facts are there will always be bad people in the World who wish to hurt others.

Most people do need medication or therapy to help them overcome their trauma and issues, there is nothing wrong with that. You need to do what works for you and trust me you may try multiple times and multiple avenues to seek help out of this darkness but the thing to remember is you keep trying, you keep moving forward because I promise you there is light, there are better days ahead. There is always tomorrow, there is always hope, there is always lightness ahead. This too shall pass is a helpful mantra to have as a tool. Or find your own Positive saying to remind you when you are feeling low.

- This too shall pass
- This is just a moment, not a lifetime
- I am stronger each and every day
- I am a survivor not a victim
- I will survive

- I am a strong person
- Or choose from hundreds of others, do a quick online search for positive quotes.

There are many forms of treatment that may help assist you on your journey. (I am not a medical professional, so please seek expert help from qualified professionals where needed). This is a basic list to give you some ideas to start with. As always do your research and find what works for you. Everyone is different.

- Counselling
- Meditation
- Mindfulness
- Journaling / Diary
- Survivors groups / women's circles
- Holistic healing techniques – massage, Reiki, Kinesiology etc
- Walking / exercise
- yoga

I can advise from personal experience though – those drugs / or alcohol / or food are only part time escapes from your reality. They might make you feel good for a little while, but the high becomes harder and harder to chase the more you get into the addiction.

The only real way to recover from trauma is to take the big deep breath and walk headfirst into it.

Be gentle with yourself.

Seek appropriately trained people to help you.

- Counsellors trained in abuse survival/ trauma
- Psychologists
- Through your GP you can get access to a Mental Health care plan that allows you to get some of the above services for free or at reduced costs.

The darkness can take you years to overcome or months- there is no time frame, there are no guidelines on how to move past this time in your life. Just KNOW you do move past it; it does not stay with you forever. And please don't get me wrong here, you will have moments and you will have recurring issues dealing with your Trauma, but nothing ever again will be as bad as that actual moment it first happened, that moment when your power was taken from you, that moment your life changed forever.

Yet remember here – **you SURVIVED that**, you faced that, and anything afterwards is healing and reaching for your power back. I am certainly not under playing

You WILL regain your power, you
WILL regain your self-esteem, you
WILL regain your self-confidence,
you WILL feel empowered once again.
You will feel love and be loved.

the effect the event has had on your whole life. There is no part of yourself, and your life not effected by the trauma. In my own experiences, it has affected my relationships with my Parents, My husband, My son, family, and friends.

So, keep going, keep striving, keep knowing that you will rise again. You WILL regain your power, you WILL regain your self-esteem, you WILL regain your self-confidence, you WILL feel empowered once again. You will feel love and be loved. You will feel respect and be respected. You will feel empowered and powerful. You will feel confident and be self confident.

Honour the process, honour the way forward. I know it is hard when you are in that darkness and trust me some 40 plus years after my first experience I still get bogged down in moments of darkness. What is different now is I know the signs, I know the feelings, and I have methods at my disposal to work my way through it. My intention is that this book will give you some tools to help you as well.

As I stated before I am not a medical professional – I am a survivor of historic sexual abuse. I am a holistic consultant. I am a Women's wellbeing coach. So let me help you. Let me show you some things that helped me heal or tools I found along the way, over my 40-year journey so far.

You are tougher than you think, and we are all tougher than we give ourselves credit for. I myself didn't think I was so strong until I started to write this all down and then realised one day – WOW I had all that happen to me, and I am still here, still standing, I have overcome my demons, overcoming my self-sabotage (mine is food), has also been alcohol in the past. Yet here I am a fully functioning Women (well a functioning woman), working full time, running my own business, being a Wife, A Mother, and a Grand Mother, a friend and numerous other entities that make up ME. Damn girl you are one strong Warrior women. It has taken me all this time to be able to look at myself in the mirror and say that and FEEL that.

So, are you ready to let me help you to also feel this in your life again?

To feel the power, to feel stronger, to feel like your old self again. To find YOUR voice again.

You WILL stand again in your power.

You WILL rise again like a
Phoenix from the ashes.

You WILL overcome these memories
and feelings from your past.

You will be whole again.

I promise you this, one day soon you will feel the same, you will be able to do the same and that moment. The one little moment in time when you take back your full power and step into your own, is so worth it. It is such a life changing and momentous moment.

You WILL stand again in your power.

You WILL rise again like a Phoenix from the ashes.

You WILL overcome these memories and feelings from your past.

You will be whole again.

So let us start this journey forward, let us join hands (so to speak) and allow me to aid you in moving yourself towards your power and your full potential.

I will not be doing the work for you, however. We will be embarking on this journey together and I will assist you all the way. ONLY YOU can do the work here though.

So, take my hand now and allow me to help lead you out of the darkness and back into your light.

Or you can put the book down now and stay as you are, keep your life in the status quo or the same. That is the power of empowerment – it is making your own choice for yourself.

It is discernment and judging for yourself what is right for you.

This book is a guide only, you choose what works for you and you alone choose what to do with the information. Some things in here will resonate with you and others will not. You choose. You decide. Start to become your own inner detective and research and search for your own information.

What is best for you?

Some things in this book will challenge you, they will upset you, they will make you scream, yell, cry and want to explode. That is all part of the journey.

Yes, it is challenging. Yet 100% worth it – I promise you.

You may decide to read through the entire book and decide for yourself if it will be helpful.

You may decide to put it down now and let it sit on your shelf for a few months / years.

You may decide that to hell with it all NOW is the time to deal with this once and for all and move on.

Whatever YOU decide is right for YOU.

It is not up to anyone else.

This is YOUR journey and only YOU
alone can decide how it plays out.

That is the first step to regaining
your EMPOWERMENT.

Step ONE

STOP judging yourself and comparing yourself to others. You are unique, a one of a kind. What may work for others – may not work for you.

CHAPTER TWO

Losing Your Power – the Event/s

Do you remember the first time you felt powerless, was it one event that took this from you, or multiple events over time?

Was it years of abuse or one moment / event?

Was it one person who took it from you or multiple people?

Whatever your story it is YOUR story and no one person will have the same experiences or way of dealing with it -that is OK. There is no judgement here, not even from yourself to you.

Leave all judgement here please.

For some it is blocked away for some time and then something in the future happens and triggers the memories, the flash backs to the original event. This can be quite traumatic as you think and feel like you are going crazy. This is when it is imperative to seek professional help. To delve into this in a place of safety and assistance with someone who can guide you through it. For others there is always that memory of the event, as clear and vivid as if it were yesterday. A place, smell, taste, music, or object that takes you back there in an instant. Other memories never really come back clearly. There is a feeling or just a "knowing" that something happened. Personally, I have both experiences. I have one very clear to this day memory of being molested by a family member, being molested by two boys in school, or a boyfriend trying to rape me and of being raped during a drunken night of what started as consensual sex and turned into something else entirely.

Yet the memories of being abused as a young child – are not clear, there are flashes, flickers of things, a certain knowing and feelings – but no real clear picture or memories of events. He has whispered in my ear as an adult that it was all our little secret – so I know he knows what he did. That just cemented things for me – because honestly there is that doubt, there is always that nagging little voice asking – did I imagine this…? Did I somehow make this up…? (Although not sure why anyone would do that…) but the doubt is more the perpetrators way of controlling the situation still. It keeps them in control – it keeps them empowered if we doubt it all. For me personally I think I just can not deal with the reality of what happened to me and how young I was and who it was that did this to me. Who it was that stole my childhood innocence.

I have consciously decided not to name my perpetrators here, that is my personal choice. I have my own very personal and very private reasons for doing that. Which I understand are contradictory given I am now writing this book about my experiences. However, that is just it. I am writing about my experiences; it should not matter what the perpetrators' names are. That is my power.

Yet this book has always been about healing and moving forward from abuse, it was not ever meant as a name and shame. Maybe a few years ago at the heart of my counselling sessions, I would have gladly screamed their names out loud. I now come from a space of knowing I do not need to do that. They know what happened, I know what happened, my Husband and my son believe me and that is all that really matters to me. You deal with your events as you see fit. That is personal empowerment.

I have a very close personal friend who is currently in the middle of a court case, having taken her abuser and the church he belongs to, to court and I fully support her. I have another friend who doesn't speak about her abuser or acknowledge him in any way, she chooses to treat him as a non-entity in her life, she has never had counselling and chooses not to talk about her abuse...I fully support her too. Because I firmly believe you deal with your issue as best works for you.

Regardless of how you remember your event the one thing that is the same is the feeling of hopelessness, or being out of control, of worthlessness. That is the moment you lost your power. I am not talking about fighting back and being able to control the situation because the fact is for various reasons you could not. You were a child fighting off an adult, or a physically weaker person fighting Off a stronger person – physically. Or a mentally controlling, nasty person controlling the situation. Or a million other scenarios.

The situation was out of your control. You cannot go back and change it. You can only move forward and fix it. Repair the damage that was done to you. It's always amazed me how we as humans get a physical injury, we cut our finger for example, so we go and clean it up and put a band aid over it to allow it to heal. Yet when we are damaged emotionally, we tend to withdraw within ourselves and don't really talk about it with many, we are hesitant to seek professional help, some never do. There is a generation of survivors who won't discuss things because – well you should just get over it...!!!

Wow if I had a dollar for every time, I have heard that line. I would be cruising the Caribbean on my private yacht right now.

For myself personally I have had several different scenarios of abuse (molestation and rape) the one thing they all have in common was my reaction to them. I froze. I did nothing. WOW did this take some therapy to move through. I beat myself up over that one thing for years. Why didn't I fight back? Why did I do nothing? Why did I freeze? Why didn't I yell or scream or kick or something, anything!! The truth to this day I don't really know. It is what I did the first time I was abused, so in subsequent events I did the same. I learnt from a young age to literally leave my body. Physically I was there, emotionally not even in the same room, I went off somewhere safe – in my mind anyway. This is known as disassociation and is a well-documented phenomena. It is how us as humans deal with trauma that is too bad for the mind to reconcile with. We literally take ourselves out of the issue.

Google – Disassociation – Disconnection and lack of continuity between thoughts, memoires, surroundings, actions, and identity.

This led to me forgetting for 20 plus years my original abuse at a young age. It only came to light again, when at the age of 26, I was seeing a therapist to deal with my molestation at age 11. I had been seeing her for several weeks about being molested at 11 years old. I remember this incident clearly to this day. Exactly as it happened, like I am still there.

During my sessions I started to have flashbacks of another room and another time, I was a lot younger and there was another person in the room. At first, I couldn't really reconcile what I was seeing or getting glimpses of. There are still a lot of blanks and things I can't remember; it is also not as clear as my other memories. I think due to who it was and my age, I just block it to help myself deal with things.

So, it is not uncommon for us to forget events and beat ourselves up over our reaction to events or how we handle things now or back then. In fact, beating ourselves up is the one thing we do best. I bet you are the same, if something goes wrong, the first thing you say to yourself is "what did I do" "how could I have done that better" or if you have been controlled you doubt, second guess and wonder about everything – we are great at this as survivors. We are always looking to please others. We want others to be happy with us, to like us, to accept us – because we can't do any of that for ourselves now can we.

Let me ask you,

Do, you like yourself?

Do you accept yourself?

Are you happy with yourself?

Because depending on where you are on your healing journey – these answers will change over time, moving forward.

At first when you start to look at your abuse to start your healing journey. You will answer no to all those questions.

Over time and with a lot of work I promise you, you will learn to like yourself and see yourself as the stronger, courageous person that you are.

During your event – what ever it was that happened to you. You felt and were made to feel powerless, voiceless, worthless, and totally not worthy of being treated decently. You were treated as an animal by an animal – can you see the irony there. We are made to feel powerless by someone who is not even in their own power. They feel worthless so they abuse you. They feel powerless so they abuse you. You give them their power – because they steel if from you to feed theirs. That is the vicious, insidious cycle of abuse. Let's break that cycle, lets change that right here and right now by taking back our power, leaving them with none of it. Because although they may have tried – they DID NOT WIN. They did not because we are survivors, and we can stand tall and proud and say a big F&*& you to them now.

They are nothing!

They are weak!

They are worthless!

I AM A SURVIVOR, NOT A VICTIM.

I AM A SURVIVOR, NOT A VICTIM.

I AM A SURVIVOR, NOT A VICTIM.

They are powerless now because we now stand in our POWER, and you WILL NOT DEFEAT ME.!!

You are a SURVIOVOR, not a victim.

I want you to repeat that with me, say it loud and proud and believe it.

I AM A SURVIVOR, NOT A VICTIM.

I AM A SURVIVOR, NOT A VICTIM.

I AM A SURVIVOR, NOT A VICTIM.

That is OUR POWER, taking back our voice, taking back our ability to stand up and say NO.

Saying that it is not OK to be beaten down and disempowered, but now you are taking back that power and control for yourself, by yourself.

You are empowering yourself to heal and move forward, step by step, inch by inch, day by day.

Just be gentle and loving to yourself.

There is no sprint here, there is no rush, you will do what you need to do as you need to do it.

In your time and on your terms.

Little by little you WILL take back control of your life. I promise you that.

There is no one to compete with, there is no race to the end.

Just do things in your own time and at your own pace.

Sometimes you will want to jump in and move through things. Other times you will want to crash out on the couch and binge watch TV, whilst downing a packet of crisps or a family block of chocolate or a bottle of wine – well you get the picture.

Whilst I do not encourage the overuse of alcohol or food in your healing. I understand the need to numb yourself at times too. I have certainly been there. Does it help NO. Not long term, not even short term really. It just masks the emotions for a while until they return again – bigger, better, stronger.

There are times when you will need to just – turn the world off for a moment. This is important on your healing journey too, as it is about taking back your power and control. Part of that is acknowledging those times you need some down time. Take a deep breath

You are empowering yourself to
heal and move forward, step by
step, inch by inch, day by day.

Just be gentle and loving to yourself.

before you move forward again. Putting yourself first is not selfish, it is very empowering.

That took me years to come to terms with, because we are conditioned from childhood – to put others first. To not be selfish. Especially women. We are taught that men are our superior or rich people are better than us, or movie stars / TV stars / Singers / Athletes are all somehow superior to us. You see where I am going here.? We are conditioned to put others above and before us. So there is a lot to undo here, I get it. Honestly these are things I still struggle with at times in my life too.

Step TWO

Book yourself some me time, a massage, a healer, a naturopath – something just for you.

CHAPTER THREE

Healing, the Journey Forward

The journey forward although the longer journey, is the most rewarding and healing.

It will be the most emotional fight of your life, the most challenging thing you have ever done and possibly ever will do.

Yet you can do it. You will get up every day and put one foot in front of the other and move forward. You will have days where you won't. You might want to curl up in a ball and sob like a baby uncontrollably, you might be tempted to drink yourself to oblivion, you may eat yourself into a constant food coma, you might get involved with drugs, you might socialise with the wrong people, you may become a workaholic, or shopaholic, you will punish yourself, you will self-sabotage, you might be in abusive relationships or allow yourself to be controlled by others, you will do an endless array of things to erase the image and the memories, anything and everything possible to block out the pain, to push down those memories – anything to avoid the one thing you do not want to do.

LOOK AT THE ISSUE...

Yet you know what – you can't avoid things forever. Well, you can but then you just keep chasing your tail and ending up right back where you are now. You know by now none of these things help for long, if really at all. They are just methods to avoid the inevitable.

It happened, it occurred, and you can't erase those memories or feelings no matter how hard you try. You have been trying, is it working? Be honest with yourself here.

You can however learn to manage them and deal with it to a certain degree, so it doesn't invade every waking moment of your life. The one thing you never do is FORGET. No matter what anyone tells you. Look back, you have tried right...? You have abused yourself, abused your body – mind – spirit and guess what – the memories are still there.

I have learnt over many years to forgive my abusers; (this does take time, however you will get to a point at some stage where you might forgive some things but not others, we are each on our own journey here. You may NEVER forgive and that is fine too) I have not ever forgotten any of the events. I am still angry at times, and sad at others.

"Just get over it", how many times have you heard that - it is so dis-empowering all over again. It is saying the event wasn't worth our attention, the event is in the past so just move on. It could not be oversimplified more if they tried. Just get over it to me gets me angry. It is telling me all over again I am not worthy of expressing myself. It really hits a raw nerve with me, as you can probably tell by now.

If "just getting over it" was so easy, then why did the numbers of suicides for post war survivors increase. Why did the number of alcoholics increase, why did the number of marriage separations increase, why did the number of domestic violence incidents increase? YEP because "just getting over it" does not work.

We deserve to be heard, we deserve to heal, we deserve better than we have had so far. We all have a right to feel safe and be safe.

Getting help, seeking out professional help is not a weakness, it is a powerful healing thing to do and your way forward to empowerment.

Don't put a time on it, just start and see where it leads. It can take years or months, it doesn't matter. The only thing that matters now is healing. This is your journey. Your gateway to again finding your voice and your power. I cannot begin to tell you how amazing it feels to stand in your own power once again and know that no matter what hand you have been dealt, you are a strong, courageous survivor and that my friend is your greatest power.

Feeling empowered is not about you putting on a superhero outfit and standing proud. It is subtler and gentler. It is that moment you can look at yourself in the mirror and say, "hey I like you", or "I love you" or "You are awesome".

I am not here to sugar coat the journey. It is tough, it is confronting, it is raw, and it is emotional. Yet having said all that it is 100% worth it.

I remember my counsellor once telling me in a session "oh you will forgive your abuser eventually" and I was sitting there thinking "you must be f*&&^%$ kidding me", there is just no way that will ever happen. I was still so angry and raw and in so much emotional pain, that I could see no way ever in my future for that to happen.

Now I stand in a room with my abusers, and they are non-people to me. Some of My abusers were family members so at times I do have to be in social situations with them. Luckily for me now I moved far far away from them so don't have to do this as much....and when I say HAVE TO, I of course have a choice. My choice is not to allow them to see they almost broke me, so I stand there almost in defiance to prove to them I did survive, they did not break me and that I am tougher and stronger than they will ever be. So that is my Power.

That is not for everyone, and I understand that – you do what is right for you.

As I was not believed by most of my family – they choose a path of let's ignore it and pretend it did not happen. Yes, I belong to a family of ostriches – that is a whole other book let me tell you. That stiff upper lip, that very British way of "Do not talk about it, do not acknowledge it, lock it away in a cupboard and ignore it. Oh and God forbid we should actually talk about our feelings, our emotions, or our dirty little secrets. That very British trait of "carry on regardless"

Yet I am sure there are a lot of you reading this who can relate. Not everyone will understand you, not everyone will believe you. Do not let that change your dialogue, because fundamentally that is their issue not yours. You know your truth; you know what happened...that is all that matters.

I also now realise a lot of what I dealt with and saw was emotionally damaged adults who could not or would not or have not dealt with their own childhood issues. Sexual abuse / Domestic Abuse / Alcoholism all seem to be hereditary in my family dynamic to some degree sadly. Good old ancestral trauma at play here folks. (loads of books and stuff on Google about this topic (ancestral Karma) if you are interested)

I stand in my power, and I have the ones who know me and love me and believe me and that means more to me than those who can't or won't believe me. That is their journey not mine. I know this must all sound over simplified, but it has taken many years of counselling and soul searching to get to this place where I stand in my power and will not let any of them take my power from me again.

Does this mean I am healed; I am over it. Hell No. I still have my moments. I still get triggered by things / people / events / places. However, what I do have now

Feeing empowered is that moment you can look at yourself in the mirror and say, "hey I like you", or "I love you" or "You are awesome".

is the ability to see these triggers and the tools to help me deal with them.

I am a firm believer in Karma and trust me Karma has dealt my abusers their fair share. I am personally not out for justice or retribution (I once was), yet I don't begrudge anyone who seeks their day in court. We all need to deal with things as we see fit and with what works for us. There is not a one cure for all. Whatever you need to do to take your power back, I encourage 100%.

As I have stated several times over the past few chapters, there is no one story fits all here. There are not two stories that are the same, there are no two ways of dealing with the abuse that are the same and there are certainly no two ways of dealing with your abusers that are the same.

You DO WHAT IS RIGHT FOR YOU and you alone. That is all you can do. That is YOUR personal power – Empowerment.

I personally have gone back and forth with counselling throughout the years, because honestly at times in my life I just wanted it all to go away and needed a break from it all. I soon learnt it never goes away and it is always just under the surface. So, the sooner we face our demons and deal with it the better. I personally now meditate and have a deep belief in a bigger force at work and no not the G_O_D word as I struggle with that one. I have had several different counsellors over my journey, starting with a sexual abuse therapist and also I have seen phycologists and counsellors, as well as holistic healers.

I also journal and for me this is my best method, just that freeing feeling of writing all my thoughts and feelings down with no judgement or recriminations. No one else will ever see it, and I can put things in there I would not necessarily tell other people. Some people find exercise works for them, or cooking, or creative endeavours. Whatever you find that works for you to express yourself in your power.

I am now working to help other people to find themselves and help them heal, and most importantly find their power again – I honestly believe that is what I was put on this earth to do, that everything I have gone through has led me here.

You DO WHAT IS RIGHT FOR YOU
and you alone. That is all you
can do. That is YOUR personal
power – Empowerment.

When you are in the depths of despair and dealing with reliving your abuse in whatever form it took, you will find it hard to see the upside or see the future as anything positive and happy. Yet I can assure you – there is an upside, there is a happy place, there is a positive future awaiting you.

Let me help you find it.

Let me help guide you back to your POWER.

Let me help you find your true self again.

So, your first assignment for lack of a better term or Step Two – I want you to make an appointment with a counsellor / therapist if you are not already seeing someone. At the same time get yourself a journal. This can be as simple as an exercise book from the local stationary supplier or as glorious as a leather bound book of secrets type diary.

Then I want you to write, doodle, draw, express your true feelings in it every day. If you are worried about someone else reading it or seeing it. Use your computer / iPad / etc and have a password protected folder, just for this purpose or keep your diary somewhere only you know.

I personally LOVE the feel of handwriting my thoughts and doodles and pictures. I also find at times as I am guided to Automatic writing – this is the best format for me. You do what is right for you and what works. Make it is basic or as intricate as you like. It is yours and yours alone.

Do you remember those days as a teenager (those of us of a certain age) where we covered our school diaries in magazine photos, stickers, drew on them etc – I want you to do this again. Make it your own.

Remember also as I stated earlier in this book, if you go and see your GP you can access a Mental health plan that will help you to get medications and treatment options for free or reduced costs. Also, if you are officially diagnosed as suffering from PTSD (trust me many now are) you can gain further assistance from various government-based options.

Step THREE
Make an appointment with your GP or Counsellor.

CHAPTER FOUR

Bad Days, and There Will Be Many, and Some of My Story

I was molested by a family member at 11 years old, he touched my private parts whilst asking me if I had a boyfriend and what had we done together. Instead of screaming at him "you friggen creepy sick bastard" I ran away. Leaving my younger sister and brother to come home to him, as he had sent them to the shop – not my finest hour, not my proudest moment. BUT I was in fight or flight mode, and I choose flight at that moment – in stunned shock and disbelief. This was someone I looked up to and respected. Someone my parents felt safe enough with to leave him looking after all three of us – aged 11 – 10 and 6 at the time. He was MY FAMILY for f&^% sake, I should be safe with him – RIGHT...? WRONG. And that is the sad fact and reality I learnt much later on - MOST assaults of a sexual nature on females, are from a male known to them.

You would think that that experience was the worst for the day right – and sadly it was bad but not the worst I experienced on this particular day. For you see later that evening when my mother was saying goodnight to me in my bed, I decided to tell her what had happened, what her brother had done to me and how I felt about it. I expected as a naive 11-year-old girl, the eldest in my family that she would take me into her arms and lovingly embrace me and tell me we would sort it out and how she and my dad would fix this. OH BOY was I wrong – NOPE what I got instead was a slap across the face and told in no uncertain terms to "not tell such disgusting lies about her brother". UMMMMMMM WTF. Yep, so right there, right at that moment my life changed forever. That very moment I realised I had NO ONE I could trust, no one I could turn to, and no one who believed me. And yes now as an adult and after a lot of soul searching and work on myself with counselling and other healing methods, I can see now that this was her being majorly triggered by this event happening to her daughter and obviously something similar had happened to her too – HOWEVER let me tell you as an 11 year old child – this has had the most profound effect on my whole entire life.

I recently brought it to her attention again, she whole heartily denied she reacted like that and says she can not remember the event. Does she believe me about my uncle nope I do not believe so. She says she is sorry if this is what happened to me – YEP great thanks Mum – IF this is what happened to me. UMMMM exactly why would I say this, where would I get this idea, where would I find this story to tell you...?? If it was not true. So yes, as you can tell I am still shocked at her to this day. I am no longer angry – well not as angry as I have been at times. Yet shocked and disturbed by it all – yes, still to this day. However, I now have the tools to deal with things that trigger me, or to be able to stop, step back and analyse what is going on for me.

At 16 I had a drug and alcohol fuelled male acquaintance hold a fully loaded shotgun to my head. Now I could have stood up to him and said he was an idiot and put that thing down, but I didn't I sat quite still and peaceful, I laughed with him, and it was in reality only two minutes which to me felt like two hours, he calmly walked away and put the gun away. Where some other acquaintances stepped in and unloaded it and put it well out of harm's way. Sometimes you have to say and do nothing to protect yourself and sometimes others around you. However, at some stage you have to stand up and say something. I unfortunately never had the opportunity with that particular idiot, and we fell out of touch, and I have no idea where he is or if he is still even alive, and no real inclination to find out either - understandably.

I worked for 21 years (the worst part being the last 10 years I was there) within a male dominated, misogynistic industry and for the most part I kept my mouth shut to what was going on around me and too me. To the downfall of my own mental health. It was a role I loved and was good at, yet in an industry that did not value me or appreciate me or my input. Well to be perfectly honest with you, did not value females or their unique perspective or inputs. At least once a week I would hear from my own Male Manager – "if she is the right man for the job" in reference to a female being promoted within the organisation. To say this organisation has a very poor history of holding onto powerful, smart, intelligent women is an understatement. Over the past few years, like the Government they have been on a recruiting drive to employ and keep females within the organisation – whilst still having the same misogynistic males as heads of the organisation – talk about a crazy situation and one that is sadly not alone.

These are just some of my many events throughout my life that have helped to build and shape me into the women I now am. It has been a long painful journey at times. Yet even now I wouldn't change a thing. Because it is who I am, and it made me who I am. Has there been blood, sweat and tears – HELL YER..! Has there also been moments of immense pride, determination, and joy – ABSOLOUTELY.!

Sadly, there will be bad days, that is just a fact. You have already had these. This is nothing new for you.

So here in this chapter are some ways to help you deal with these a bit differently from how you might have done previously. You may have heard that old saying – you only know what you know, and you can only do what you do with what you know at the time. So please – do not beat yourself up for not knowing any different. That is what life is all about – learning and growing.

Bad days can look like, yet are certainly not limited to...

Also read up on subjects around PTSD and "fight or flight" that will shed some more professional light on these listed below, as well.

- I can't be bothered
- I don't want to get out of bed
- I can't deal with anything today
- I can't stop crying
- I am angry but unsure why
- I crave food / alcohol / sex/ love etc.
- I am fat, ugly, dumb, useless etc insert numerous negative words....
- No one understands me
- Depression
- Anxiety

How to deal with each of these.

First be gentle on yourself and NO JUDGEMENT here. Sit with it for a minute and tune into what is really going on. Grab a coffee / water / herbal tea (no alcohol or soft drinks) and sit outside if you can or in your room – somewhere you feel safe. Even in the shower (without the coffee obviously) but just focus your attention inside.

- What is really going on.
- Feel and connect with whatever first comes to mind when you ask this.
- What is the trigger, was it something said, did, felt…?
- Tune into the emotions and dig deep into it to see what is really going on and what was the trigger to you feeling this way.?

Depression, what is behind this…? Is this sadness, anger, medical condition or other? Depression is such a large range of emotions, feelings, and symptoms. It can be helped by medical interventions, however (and please note here (I am not a medically trained Doctor)) Some medical conditions require proper medical diagnosis and treatment. you can also deal with the symptoms without medical intervention. There are numerous options here to help from herbal remedies, therapies, talking to people who suffer the same. The hardest thing I always find is revealing myself to others, I have such a huge issue around this – I think no one will understand, no one cares, no one has lived my experiences. Yet each and every time I 100% find talking about this eases the pain and another person's point of view can often help me see things differently. There is an old saying – "A problem shared is a problem halved"

I can' be bothered, lack motivation, this is a Biggy because it is where we really need to dig deep to deal with ourselves at our rawest. Ask yourself what can I do that will bring me joy right now? Do not judge this, just go with it, it might be something as simple as laying on the couch watching a movie or downing a whole block of chocolate – whatever it is that is ok. Not all the time though. Sometimes this simply lasts a few hours or a day or two. When it is longer or more sustained look at medical or alternative options. Seek help.

I don't want to get out of bed, why is staying here the better option. If it is ok then why can't I just stay here all day, how does that make me feel? Who am I letting down if I stay here? What am I achieving staying here, no judgement? It is perfectly ok to stay in bed some days if you have no responsibilities or can get others to help you here.

I can't deal with anything today, OK so why not, what is stopping you, what is the fear / feeling here. Tune into this and journal or meditate on this further. Sometimes we just need to stop the merry go round of life and step off for a little while, that is ok. No judgement. When you get like this, nature or water can help soothe you.

I can't stop crying, sometimes this is literally about releasing the emotions around the things you are

Journal your results, take time to
tune into the emotions and write
it all down. It is all part of the
journey to becoming whole again.

remembering and healing from. Please do not be too hard on yourself here. Allow the tears, be honest with those around you about feeling low and blue and being teary. Pack the tissues. Again, no judgement.

Imagine you are a volcano and every now and again it needs to erupt and spew lava (tears) in order to release that build up of pressure. If you do not manage the release – it will become uncontrollable and be a major eruption.

I am angry …. ok deep dive into why, again this can be releasing emotions around your issues. These are genuine and real emotions. Be honest with yourself. Tune into the anger. What are you angry about? Who are you angry with – and sometimes this can be yourself? That is an interesting part of the journey. I used to feel angry with myself all the time about the way I was dealing with things, or how I judged myself or others...Yep beating myself up some more because that is always fun (insert sarcasm). Berate myself before others do.

Journal your results, take time to tune into the emotions and write it all down. It is all part of the journey to becoming whole again. I often look back at some of my old journals to see how far I have come and what I have learnt about myself over the journey. It can be hugely rewarding to see how far you have come.

Also treat yourself, give yourself credit for the work you are doing. Shout yourself a massage or lunch out with a friend etc...whatever it is to give yourself a reward for the hard work. Even just a walk along the beach / park etc, it doesn't have to cost a fortune to give back to yourself. You and you alone are the most important person in your life right now.

- Do not expect everyone else to see things as you do, how could they, these are your thoughts, ideals, emotions, experiences etc. No one else sees things like you do. However, do not sit in this alone either, it helps to talk about your feelings and share your emotions and experiences with the right people / person.

- Sometimes we need to be alone to work it out for ourselves, other times we need someone who understands to talk things through with.

- Sometimes you will need some time out or down time. So, get someone to watch the kids / pets and take yourself off for a few hours / days, to sit and be just by yourself. Write down your feelings / thoughts / insights. Talk to

YOU do matter.

YOU are worthy.

YOU do deserve better.

YOU are awesome.

Keep going. Do not give up.

family / friends / professionals. Do what you need to do to cope.

Sometimes life becomes so overwhelming and suffocating and you can't see anyway out or anyway forward. These are the times you need to stop and focus on you.

What do you need right now?

What do you want right now?

How can someone else help you right now?

Because at the end of the day,

YOU do matter.

YOU are worthy.

YOU do deserve better.

YOU are awesome.

Keep going. Do not give up.

Step FOUR

Book some YOU time.

Tools to Assist

Counselling – Once you have acknowledged your trauma / issue / experience this is always the first and, in my opinion, best place to start. Speaking with a trained and qualified counsellor, who can see things from a different perspective, who can help you to see things for a new angel. Someone with the tools and skills necessary to help you dig deep and really look into the eye of the storm that is your trauma and more importantly help you start the journey to healing. To begin to live a life that is of your choosing again. Not just going through the motions as some sort of robot on automatic pilot, who is lost in a world of emotions and grief and anger and regrets and a million other emotions that keep you awake at night and in a dream state during the day. Is this all sounding familiar...?

Group sessions – When you are ready and this for some might be straight away and for others much later down the path. For me personally it is something I resisted for a very long time and regretted that decision once I started attending a group. Because the fact is – even though we feel like we are alone at times, and like no one else could possibly understand – the very sad truth and reality is, there are so many people out there like us who have experienced untold grief and harm. Once you start talking you find so many who get you, so many who feel like you do, so many who share your pain. It is both comforting and sad to see and hear all these other stories too.

Mediation – Again this is something you might like to do not long after your experiences or something you come to later on in your healing journey. It is something for me that brings relief and just a few precious moments of peace, where I can connect with myself and experience that stillness, that mindfulness, that Zen moment. Do I feel this all the time – (laughing as I write this) No it is not, I still have moments where I can not still my mind, where I think about the shopping list, or what is for dinner or the to do list in my head......so yes it is also an ongoing journey for me. Yet no judgement here just fact, because I am not a monk, I do not sit in stillness for hours or days at a time. I am a human being with real life issues and my mind is still learning to stop and be still at times.

Confronting the person / persons – this is also a personal choice and for some not even an option, so I have included it here for those who need or want to and for those who can. Other than my Parents I have never felt the need for myself personally to confront any of my abusers. I have watched as Karma had her say with some, I have lost touch with others, so have no idea and to be honest I just no longer have that inkling to do so. How did it go when I confronted my Parents – well you have read how it went with my Mother. She has since suffered two strokes and so we do not discuss anything that is too upsetting because I just don't care really to be honest. I know the truth – I know what happened and is she can't or won't see then I can do nothing to make her. As far as my father and his abuse of me as a child (which I have not written about in this book) I spoke to him once and he denied it all and threatened legal action against me if I continued to slander his good name (LOL Good name – yer righto) However at the dead of my grand father whilst we were all standing around at my Aunties house grieving and remembering he put his arm around my shoulders and whispered into my ear that "it was all our little secret hey and no one else needs to hear my version of events"

So, this is where I tell you that confronting your abuser is entirely up to you and this is your power. However what I will say is PLEASE do not expect an apology or any form of acknowledgement, go in expecting nothing and then you will not be disappointed or upset when you get nothing. You may be one of the lucky few who gets the heartfelt sorrow and apology and I really hope you do. Just do not expect it and then you won't be hurt again. It is all about discernment and power – YOUR power to choose. Your power to make this decision. Your power to know your truth and not need anyone else's acknowledgement.

Retreats / Time out / time away – these can be many and varied so choose wisely and do your homework. If choosing a retreat, what kind of retreat is it? If choosing to take time out, let people know where you will be and when you are likely to return so that someone is aware of where you are. Taking time out and away to look at things and heal can be very cathartic. It can be very emotional and very cleansing so choose your options wisely here, for what you need, what YOU want to achieve and what YOU want to do here.

Journalling / Diary – I am a HUGE journal writer, most days I am filling pages in my journal of random life stuff. For me it is my way of clearing it out of my head and putting it down on paper. No one else reads it and no one else sees it. If you are worried about that, then look it away somewhere safe, or regular burn it during a full moon ceremony, to help clean and clear away the old energies. I write about many and varied stuff, things that are happening in my life, things that are happening in the world, spiritual stuff, good things, bad things and all in between. I draw pictures at times or add things to the pages. It is yours to do with and write what you want, that is the joy of it all. I even sometime do some automatic writing and let things fly out as they see fit. I am still old school here and I do write it all down with pen and paper rather than on a computer. I did try the computer option, but for me (as someone who did not grow up with computers) I felt that I needed the pen and paper option to connect better with my subconscious. So do what ever works for you. Just try it and see how you go. I often feel lost if I do not unburden my thoughts onto paper. Yes, I still talk with my family and friends, yet my journal is just that most trusted friend who listens without judgement, and let's face it we all need one of those.

Mediation – sitting down with someone not connected to you and your abuser and talking things through, telling them how you feel about things and hearing their version of things. I did not get the chance to do this in person, however I had the opportunity during some work with a counsellor to do a process where you sit in both seats. You sit in one seat and talk from your perspective and then you literally swap seats and sit and talk from the abusers perspective. For me personally this helped me to see things differently, I could see the hurt and anger on their side from their own experiences with abuse and hurt. Did it give me a grater sense of compassion and understanding – well somewhat. It certainly did not take away my hurt or anger towards them – at that time. However, I need to add here – I am a Libran and as such I do see both sides of the story and need that peace, harmony, and balance. So, for me this technique was helpful. However, I understand it may not work for everyone. Here again is where I tell you – this is YOUR journey and only YOU will know what is right for you and what is not. That is your power and your discernment.

Other things that might help

- Make your mental health and wellbeing your number one focus, this is not selfish this is selfless. Because you can not pour from an empty cup.

- Learn to notice what triggers you and then how to deal with it and let it go

Make your mental health and wellbeing your number one focus, this is not selfish this is selfless. Because you can not pour from an empty cup.

- Find a form of exercise that you like and start doing It regularly, walking, bike ride, swimming, dancing, Yoga the options here are endless and some can be done right here in your own home, so if you are someone who doesn't want to do the group thing, go solo and just get moving. I can not stress enough how important this is for your mental health wellbeing, not to mention your physical wellbeing.

- Find alternative therapy as an add on to what you are already doing. I found several things that really helped me to process trauma and issues as I was dealing with some of my most profound healings. Again, seek out what works for you, as certainly here is not a one fit fixes all. Trust yourself, you will know what works for you and what doesn't. However, be prepared for some pushback from your medical practioners here......again YOU and only YOU know what is right for you and your mind and body.

Things that will certainly NOT help.

_There is no judgement here, I also went down some of
these paths. However, I wrote this book to help you,
so you do not have to endure a lifetime of grief._

_ALL is in your hands and your power
alone. ONLY YOU can choose – choose to
deal, choose to heal, or choose to lose._

- Drugs, they may dull your pain for a little while, yet they will not dull it forever. This is a slippery slope to start down, so be prepared for your life to get worse before it gets better if you start on this road.

- Alcohol, smoking, food – any form of addictive behaviour, these all help to dull the pain and memories for a little while, however once you come down, wake up, start a new day – you soon realise that all your memories and experiences are still there, right where you left them. So why not save yourself a lot of grief and money, and just stare the trauma in the eye and say OK let's do this, lets fix this s%*& once and for all.

- Bad relationship and friends, just like the above they may help for some time. They will not and can not take away your pain and memories.

I wrote this book to help you, so you do
not have to endure a lifetime of grief.

ALL is in your hands and your
power alone. ONLY YOU can
choose – choose to deal, choose
to heal, or choose to lose.

Only you can do that. No one else can do it for you. That is one lesson that is sometimes hard to learn, as we progress on our journey.

- Workaholic, this is also an addiction and an escape habit. Working hours that leave little time for anything else. Working hours so you do not have time to look at anything, feel anything or deal with anything. Oh yes you are working to build a bigger brighter future for you and yours, yep fine I get that. However be honest here, are you doing that 100% for your family or are you somehow running, in fight or flight mode, avoiding the truth, avoiding your pain, your demons your trauma...?? Just be honest with yourself here.

- Feeling like you can or somehow should help everyone, save the world one person at a time or one animal at a time. This is fine if you yourself are healed and aware of your issues and triggers. However if you are using this to keep yourself from looking at your own issues then it becomes a problem.

Moving Forward, How, and When

Moving forward, moving away from the event, the trauma and the pain. It all sounds great right. Well, it is not really how it works.

Yes, you move forward.

Yes, you move away from the event as time moves on.

However, you can move away from the trauma and pain, you do learn to deal with it, you do learn to not have it impact your life 24/7, you do start to not think about it day and night, you do see how you are no longer triggered by events, sounds, people, places. You do see how you are healing and dealing with what happened to you. Yet you never actually forget or forgive or "get over it".

Once you start looking at counselling, or getting medical help, once you start staring your trauma and pain in the eye and saying ok let's fix this, you are starting on your journey forward. You are moving forward, because you are no longer sitting in it and letting it control you. You are taking back the power; you are taking back your control, and you are moving forward.

The how is easy, (well not easy but you know what I mean) I have written about several ways to help you to seek help, to ask for help, to start the process of healing in the previous chapter.

- Seek out medical or properly qualified people to help you. Getting a mental health care plan from your GP can be a great place to start because in some countries you are then able to access cheaper or heavily discounted services with psychologist and counsellors. (At the time or writing this book)

- Look at alternative option for health and wellbeing both mental and physical health, I strongly recommend the Holistic approach – MIND _ BODY _ SPIRIT.

- Journal or write in a diary to get your thoughts and ideas out of your head, honestly, I cannot recommend this enough.

- Find a physical activity that brings you joy; this will help with mental and physical health whilst you heal

- Join a group of likeminded, or people with similar trauma to talk about things with, if you prefer to do things alone or on your own. Join an online forum, where you can remain anonymous yet still have your say and see what others are feeling and experiencing.

- Avoid addictive people and substances as much as you can. You will find you naturally move away from the negative / toxic people and things in your life when you actively start the healing process.

- Take time out for yourself, retreat, time out, time away to help heal and nurture you at this time of healing

The when – well only you will know that. Only you will know when the time is right for you. Only you will know when you are ready, willing, and able. This is the most empowering part of the journey to be honest, because this will be for most of you the first time you take back some control over your life.

YOU choose when.

Yes, your family, friends, GP etc can all tell you It is time, geezz even I am telling you it is time in this book. Yet the reality is NONE of us can make you do something you are not ready to do. You know you best, so you will know when you are ready to start your healing journey.

For some it happens gradually and over some time, you think about it for a while then life takes over again, and you put it back on the back burner to simmer away until the next time you are willing to look at it. This can take weeks, months, or years for some depending on a lot of different factors.

For others it will be a very quick, very swift action – and wham bam before you know it you are well into your healing journey and looking the beast in the eyes.

So whatever works for you is best for you. I would not for one minute dare to sit here and write that this is an easy process, and you will breeze through it without a tear or without a breakdown or without your life being turned upside down and inside out and every other which way in between.

Take time out for yourself, retreat,
time out, time away to help heal and
nurture you at this time of healing.

NOPE – not the reality, not what will happen.

HOWEVER – I will sit here and dare to tell you that it will be the most rewarding, satisfying and life altering thing that you every do just for you. The event or events that led you to seek help changed your life forever, that is fact. That cannot be changed that is the sad reality here.

It happened.!

So, you either choose to get on with life and pretend it did not, until the time it comes creeping back somehow or someway.... OR you stare the beast down and say NOPE not going to affect my life any more I am taking back control, and the control starts with me accepting what happened and dealing with the fall out.

There will be tears, for some and even me I heard it many times. "I am scared to open that can of worms because I am not sure I will ever stop crying once I start". There is some truth to that, you will cry buckets. There will be the heart felt soul retching, deep from the inner sanctum of your self – gut renting sobs, snot pouring from your nose, uncontrollable stream of tears, and then there will be the hours of not being able to stop, and there will be the sniffing and slow tears that dry and return over and over again. I am not here to sugar coat things and pretend this is easy. It is not. Yet nothing can impact you and hurt you as much as that original incident. That first time for some or the most soul-destroying time for others. Reliving it is just that, it can not hurt you like it first did – I promise you that.

Yet at the end of your journey as you look back and with so much pride and self-satisfaction you say to yourself "I SURVIVED, I AM a SURVIOR", it will all be worthwhile. That is a powerful moment when you realise you are no longer a victim, you are a SURVIVOR. Strong and powerful and owning it.

I remember a time when I was seeing another counsellor who specialised in Childhood sexual abuse, specialising in those who had been abused by their own Fathers. (As she had been, so she knew her stuff let me tell you...) She said to me during one session, "you will one day forgive your father". Honestly, I nearly lost my breakfast right there and then. I thought you must be stark raving bonkers. Are you friggen crazy or just plain demented. Of course, all this was said in my head because even back then I was too scared to speak up too much in front of others. I left that session, and I was seeeeeething angry.......bat shit crazy angry....... ready to drive my car through her window crazy.

OK you get it I was a tad upset yep. (Triggered much here – YES)

Forgive him.... not likely.

This was my dad, my father. I had him on a pedestal– I idolised that man. You see I was 26 before I starting having flash back to when he molested me / sexually abused me as a child. I was the eldest of four – one did not survive her first year. (Which is when the abuse started – after she passed. I was 4). I was in counselling with another therapist dealing with the uncle molesting me at 11 and mum slapping my face traumatic incident, because I have never forgotten that and to this day see it all as clear as if it was yesterday.

When these therapy sessions started bringing up memories of another time and another room and other things happening to me. Apparently, I have since learnt this is also quite common. We regress memories that we find the hardest to deal with and face, those things we can not make sense of as a four-year-old child. Not everyone represses, but a lot do. Also, I was one of those children who could leave their bodies when bad things were happening to them, so it took some time and counselling for it to all start coming up to the surface. Wholly shit right, was it not bad enough my uncle molested me, and my mum didn't believe me, so she slapped my face so hard it still hurts today in my mind. Nope let's throw in some abuse from your dad as a child too over several years, just to see how strong you really are. YEP, OK then. (insert palm face slap emoji here folks).

So hence the need to see another counsellor, my first one was ok with the uncle and mum thing, but the repressed memories and dad abuse was a whole new ball game. So, she recommended me to another colleague who specialised in this form of repressed memories and abuse from a father / Parent.

So, I had two very intense years of therapy and treatment to bring the memories up and deal with them. To be honest some are still buried and we, well mostly me have decided they can stay there. I do not need to see it all to know it was a traumatic experience and one I have had to deal with and live with my whole life. However, for me it has been the most incredible journey or self-discovery and now I get to help others to heal and deal and empower them to take back control of their lives too. That for me is one of the biggest rewards for what I went through.

At the end of your journey as
you look back and with so much
pride and self-satisfaction you say
to yourself "I SURVIVED, I AM a
SURVIOR", it will all be worthwhile.

I am here to tell you it will be hard, yet it will also be so rewarding, and you will feel so empowered.

So, are you ready?

Or do you still need to wait and process, because either option is fine.

Only YOU can decide when the time is right.

However, if you are ready and now is your time then let us dive right in here and start the process.

- The very first thing I want you to do is grab a large notebook and start writing down all your memories and thought around what YOUR incident / event was. This is just for you; you will be the only one to see it and read it. If you fear someone else might see it or access it. Then you can always use a password protected word document on your computer, or keep your journey under lock and key, hidden somewhere only you have access to. It is important that you feel safe being able to write all you need to release here. This is yours and yours alone. Your thoughts, your words, your images – these are not to share with anyone else if you do not wish to.

- The second thing I want you to do is make an appointment with your medical professional to get yourself a health care plan moving forward OR make an appointment with your preferred therapist. This MUST be someone you feel safe and comfortable with. If you make an appointment and meet this therapist and do not feel safe or comfortable with them, then you DO have the right to leave and choose someone else. Sometimes it can take several times to find the right fit. This is really important that you find the right person for you. It can be confronting for those of us who have never stood up for ourselves to then stand up to a therapist that is not working for us. It is all part of the journey. Be strong.

- The third thing you need to do is book yourself **Utime**, make an appointment with yourself each week. Put this in your calendar. Time to put aside for yourself, grab a massage, go for a walk in nature – time out just for yourself without distractions. This time is to be used for You and You alone. Time to reflect and think about things. YOU TIME. This is not time to go shopping or get your hair done or nails done, or binge watch the latest on Netflix etc –

NO this is to be YOU, alone time. Somewhere you can be still and reflect, just being in the moment with yourself. Make this as important as a doctor's appointment you can't break.

CHAPTER SEVEN

Finding YOUR Power Again

What is this elusive power of which you speak here – you might be asking. Do I have some unknown superpower I am not aware of. Am I secretly a superhero under these clothes.?

Well Yes & No....

Yes, you do have undiscovered superpowers, however they are not hidden under your clothes.

They are hidden, and buried much deeper under years and layers of being told you are not enough, not good enough, worthless, unworthy of being loved, useless etc etc on and on with the negative words that have been directed at you over the years. From both those who hurt you and from yourself and your own negative self-talk/ self-doubts – Yes, we can be our own worst enemies here too with our own self-criticisms.

This one can be harder to overcome than the verbal abuse from others. No one talks to us as bad as we talk to ourselves. The negativity and self-loathing at times can be quite harsh. SO, overcoming that and quietening that inner voice can take some time and effort too.

So, when I say finding your power again – I really mean, reconnecting with **YOUR** truth, with your real self, with the you that you really are buried deep inside under all this negative talk, self-criticism, self-loathing and judgements.

You are still in there, wanting to get out. Sometimes you see flickers of the power peeking through the layers. Those moments of true peace and mindful wellbeing. Those moments where you are totally free to BE YOURSELF.

That is what I mean when I say finding your power again. It is the reconnecting with yourself, your truth, your story, your wants, your needs, your dreams, your desires.

Not what others have imposed on you with their ideals, their opinions, their beliefs, their thoughts.

Some can call this a midlife crisis or reliving your youth moment – however I feel it is much deeper than that. This is about truly getting in touch with yourself after being lost for a long time in someone else's story or version of you.

It is that "dark night of the soul" moment. Where we look at and reflect on our life so far. Then work out where we need to adjust or change course to put us back on OUR path.

You see what happens when you have been abused and/or traumatised, you disconnect with your true self. You go into fight or flight mode. There are other modes however the two basic ones are fight or flight. We either fight back against the event or we take flight and withdraw within ourselves, drugs, alcohol, food, abusive / toxic relationships, work...anything we can use to not think about who or what we really are all about.

From my own person event – I took flight, I withdrew so deeply within myself and disconnected that for 20+ years I had forgotten all about the event and what had happened to me consciously. However subconsciously

I had not, because I had become this quiet, shy, withdrawn child who was too scared to stand up and be seen, for fear of being hurt. I withdrew into myself and my own thoughts. I had imaginary friends and kept to myself; I became invisible. I did not really connect with people at Primary school / high school. I had some friends yet no one that I am still in touch with on any level today all these years later.

Even today I have very superficial relationships, I do not let people in. I keep everyone at arm's length. This is my lesson and my journey still. Yes we are all , always – works in progress.

This was my choice. I just did not trust people, but on a deeper level I felt so unworthy I could not understand why anyone would want to be friends with me anyway – so I just did not try.

Yet I do not ever remember feeling – alone. I knew I had spirit around me from an incredibly early age. I had lost me baby sister when I was four years old, and she was barely six months old. So, I always felt someone with me.

I guess on some deep level as a young child I knew from being able to retreat deep within myself to protect myself – that I was never really alone.

It may sound strange to you now reading this, however for me I was surrounded by beings. Angels, Spirit Guides, Fairies, Galactic beings – whatever you choose to call them, I had them all. I still do, they are with me always and bring me such peace and happiness. A sense of knowing who I really am with them.

Even now many, many, many years later – I always feel those Spirit ancestor energies around me still. I am always guided and protected. As funny as that may sound from someone who has experienced the constant abuse from various people in my youth.

From 4 years old until I was nine it was my father.

At 11 it was my uncle.

At 12 it was two boys from school at the local pool.

At 14 from a boyfriend who tried to force me to have sex with him.

That was my reality, which was all I knew about myself for a long time. I thought that all defined who I was. A victim, someone to be abused, someone unworthy of being loved or treated with respect. Someone to abuse and mistreat. Because I believed that – guess what it kept happening to me. Even into adulthood where I was raped by my partner when he came home drunk.

We started messing about and I was laughing as he is a funny drunk. However, things turned sexual, and he was much stronger than me and I did what I had always done and retreated into myself – so I guess he took this as consent. Straight afterwards I got up showered and left the house. I did not return for several long hours. When I did finally returned home, he was confused and looking at me what happened. We did sit down and discussed this event in detail. He is beyond apologetic and has spend the rest of our lives together making up for it. Never has he even raised his voice to me in anger since. We still have our issues and he has his problems – neither of us are perfect.(Does he still drink – Yes. That is his demon and one I am unable to fix for him, that is his journey, and I am unable to help if he doesn't want to look at his demons).

I am sure there are many people out there who can relate to this sadly. As the statistics show that I am far from being alone here. A staggering amount of people are sexually abused each year, and most by people or persons they know or are familiar with.

How we stop this and change the statistics is a whole other book and a story that will not change in my lifetime sadly. We need to move slowly and change the perception (especially amongst males) that they somehow own females/ family members / friends, or have to control, abuse, disrespect us for power and control.

By taking back our power and standing strong and tall, even after all this abuse and trauma – that is our strength. It can takes years to get to a point where you might be ready to even look at your past and more years before you choose to deal with and heal these issues.

You will go back and forth with therapy and other holistic treatments. Sadly, there is no pill to fix all this available from your local GP. They can however help with referrals to various therapy / counselling etc.

It will take all your courage to be on this healing journey, yet you will be ready and know when the time is right for you to do so.

That is the real power – the acceptance and willingness to look into the eye of the storm and say – NOPE no more. You no longer have that power over me, the power to control me through my thoughts, self-doubts, unworthy feeling – any longer. I Now am taking back my POWER. You no longer have it.!

That is the true feeling of being empowered, when the trauma, abuse, sense of victimhood no longer controls every waking thought or moment.

When you can breath a sigh of relief is just for a moment, and tell yourself and believe it that you are a SURVIVOR.

That feeling, that thought, that energy of saying that to yourself and then saying it again aloud – is A-M-A-Z-I-N-G....!

Try it – if you have not done so already.

Say it loud and say it proud.

I TAKE BACK MY POWER.

I AM NOW BACK IN CONTROL OF MY LIFE, MY THOUGHTS, MY EMOTIONS.

I AM WORTHY.

I AM POWERFUL.

I AM LOVED.

I AM A SURVIVOR!

Make it your mantra, your creed, your motto. Your go to saying to yourself each and every time you need to

I TAKE BACK MY POWER.

I AM NOW BACK IN CONTROL OF MY
LIFE, MY THOUGHTS, MY EMOTIONS.

I AM WORTHY.

I AM POWERFUL.

I AM LOVED.

I AM A SURVIVOR!

pump yourself up and feel that power and energy serge through you.

You do not have to use my words, make your own mantra that means something to you.

Even better – make it pretty and print it out and put it up all over your home in places where you can see it.

Above your bathroom mirror.

On your desk.

On your fridge.

On your wardrobe door.

On your phone / computer as a screen saver.

As a constant reminder to yourself whilst healing that you are powerful and a survivor, even after all you have been through.

That I finding Empowerment. That is the goal. (well one of many).

EMPOWERMENT – Now What?

Ummmm what does that even mean.

Are you powerful, are you a v8 engine?

What is this empowerment you speak of?

Well, my friends it is as simple as YOU BEING YOU.

100% open, honest, and real.

Not hiding in the closet fearing speaking out.

Not sitting in the corner too afraid to speak.

Not being at a family gathering and pretending everything is fine when your abuser is sitting in the same room as you pretending nothing happened. OR even choosing to not acknowledge them or the situation any more because it no longer matters to you what others think or believe.

OR even choosing not to speak up, not to say anything to others. Yet accepting and acknowledging within yourself these events happened and looking at them and seeking help from properly qualified professionals when and where necessary.

Empowerment is – you saying to yourself "Hey this happened to me, and this is how I feel about it." Whether other people believe me or not is their issue not mine.

Own your story. Own your truth. These are not fake memories or false memories or some bad dream. These are your memories, these are your moments, these things did happen to you.

It is no longer your responsibility to help soothe other people's feelings, emotions, or issues.

I am not talking about taking a knife to your abuser. That is not empowering. That is simply lowering yourself to their level. NOPE we rise above it, we ARE better than them. For the simple reason we would never do that to another human being.

I used to hear all the time – That abusers abuse. Yep, that is true a lot of the time – especially with men (research the statistics here) Most women are hardwired to be empathetic and sympathetic enough to not direct their abuse at others. (I said most – there are always the exceptions to that).

SO, empowerment is about owning your truth and still be a fully functioning, human being doing life and all that that entails.

It is not about perfection – forget that. There is no such thing. All those TV commercials selling perfection in a pill, bottle, tube, make up, power, gel, clothing etc – is 100% BS.

There is no such thing.

Perfection is the lie, it is an illusions, it is unobtainable. It is false and fake and what is subject to millions of variances depending on each persona view, tastes, likes, dislikes, social agendas – you get the drift....etc etc etc.

Just BE. Your body just is. Your skin just is. Your emotions just are. Your home. Your wardrobe. Your family. Your job. Your dog and on and on and on – Just are. None are perfect.

WHEWWWW what a relief right. Wow I can just sit back and let myself go now right. Well, no not exactly. There is always room for improvement. We might not all want to look like the latest fashionista or celebrity – but we do all want something we do not already have. Whether that is something material, physical or spiritual. I believe that it is just human nature to want more.

We all want improvement and empowerment. And that comes from within, not without – not from a pill, a dress, a house, a car, a holiday, or any other materialist object / thing.

We really need to stop comparing ourselves with others – that is our first mistake each day.

We need to be happy with what we have and who we are now, better can come for sure.

Empowerment – is being YOU. Truly – honestly – uniquely YOU and owning that and being proud of that.

SO, how does that look. Well look at someone you envy or admire.

Is this someone strong and independent. What is it you like and admire about them?

What is it about them that draws you in?

Is it their physical appearance?

Is it an energy or vibe they have?

What Is it that you admire most about them?

Now compare that to yourself. (now I know I said stop comparing yourself to others, but just bare with me here as you will see there is a method to my madness here)

Do you see these qualities within you?

Or are they lacking. Do you want to be more like them in some way.

For me personally it has always been Cher and PINK. I just love their kick arse, take no prisoners, no one F*&^^ with me attitude, powerful energy.

I do not see this within myself. I always felt so powerless and like I had to adapt and change to my environment. So, I felt like I was lacking in these qualities.

THEN I started to dig a little deeper and look at my life and I thought – whoa wait a minute here.

I have been abused, molested, raped (all before I was 16).

I have watched many family and friends die in car accidents and cancers and my sister at 6 months old.

I have been through floods and bush fires. AND I am still here, still standing, still (well reasonably) got my stuff together.

WHOLLY Sh(* I am kick arse, I am take no prisoners, I am do not F with me, I am a powerful energy. WHO KNEW.!!!!!

Have I always felt this – Hell No!!!

This is years of inner reflection, therapy, self-work, tough years, avoidance, addictions, self-loathing, procrastination (my favours thing LOL).

Years of looking into the eye of this storm that has been my life so far. (59 years as I write this now)

SO, I guess what I am trying to say here – is this is not a quick fix.

This is not something you will just "get over" one day. It takes time, it takes courage, and it takes an inner strength and determination that you will not even realise you have.

You will stop and start many times; it is a bit like dieting that yo-yo thing. You start and you are 100% committed. Then something happens and you put it on hold for a few weeks / month / years.

Then OK I am ready again now, I have picked myself up again, brushed myself off again and I am ready to do this now.

So, you start again and you are 100% committed and something happens – yes you see what I mean.

Do not be hard on yourself.

YOU are not weak, or worthless, or useless or any other of a million negative things you will call yourself.

YOU ARE NOT.

You are simply a survivor surviving.

I am still not sure when you reach that magical nirvana, where all is forgotten and forgiven, and you reach optimum inner peace.

Honestly, I am yet to find that place 100%.

What I have found is.

- I am OK with my story so far.
- I am OK with who I am.
- I am giving it my best each and every day.
- Yes, I have bad days still.
- Yes, I still fall backwards at times and that is OK.
- Life is like a roller coaster, and you have to take the ups and the downs – it's all just part of the ride.
- I am not here to please everyone, just me.
- It is OK to be slightly broken and different from everyone else.

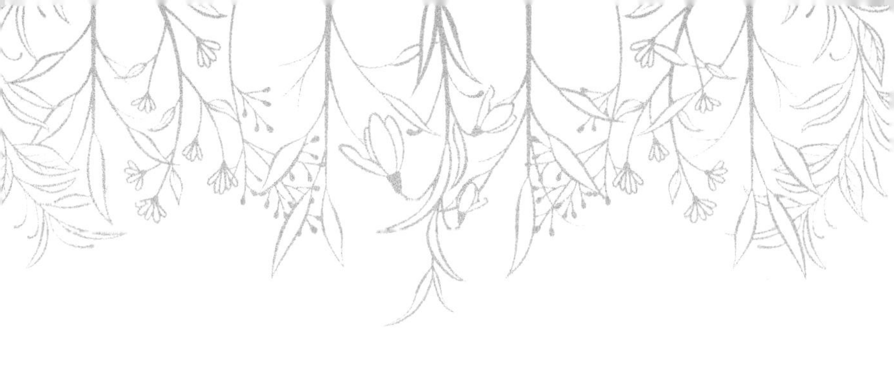

YOU are not weak, or worthless, or useless or any other of a million negative things you will call yourself.

YOU ARE NOT.

You are simply a survivor surviving.

- I AM ME!
- I AM WORTHY!
- I AM A SURVIVOR.

To Talk about My Story with Others or Not?

This is the biggest part of your journey and one of the most empowering things you can choose to do. Because ultimately that is it – this is your decision.

Only you can decide how much or what you tell others.

You can go all public and yell it from the rooftops, or you can keep it to yourself and know what happened and be happy with that, otherwise you can go halfway.

All in or all out, half in or half out. it all depends on you.

However if you do decide to go all in and tell everything - be prepared.

Not everyone will see things as you do, not everyone will understand, not everyone will be sympathise. So be prepared for the million different version of how people will react.

It hardly goes as we imagine. I remember when I finally told my mum about my dad abusing me – I stupidly or naively though she would react differently. I expected her to take me in her arms and cry and cover me with love, kisses and sympathy. Again, she couldn't deal with it, again she tried to blame me, again she pulled back and took his side. Then just to add salt to the wound I was baring – they threatened to sue me for defamation of character. Yep, me the victim, me the one hurting, me their daughter was threatened by a lawyers letter for defamation of character. I laugh now at the absurdity of this situation. And see it for what it really was, a desperate move by two desperate people – desperately holding on to the illusion of the perfect family, the perfect parents, nothing to see here folks.

I just want to warn you to be prepared. VERY VERY rarely do things turn out as we might want them too.

If you choose to go ahead with legal action and court to get your completion, you do what you need to do. However also be prepared here for backlash and people who are not ready to believe you, people who will do anything in their power to undermine you and have you questioning your own mind and your own sanity.

So I guess what I am saying here is hold strong, because you will need all your strength and determination to keep a straight and narrow here.

This chapter is about helping you decide what to do next, and to help you see all the possible outcomes here.

Personally I decided along time ago to not move forward with legal action or publicly name and shame. That was my decision at that time. I have also decided in writing this book to use a pseudonym so as to keep myself and all involved nameless. That is my decision and that is mine alone to make. I do not expect others to understand my decision, it is not theirs to understand and it is not my responsibility to explain my decision to anyone else. I would like that people would respect my decision, however I am not naive enough to know that curiosity will have people guessing and searching.

I write this book to help others on their search for peace and empowerment, I did not write it to draw attention to myself or for any sort of sympathy or understanding.

That would have obviously been the desired outcome all those many many years ago, however this was not to be my case.

I have family and friends that still to this day – can not hear what I say, can not believe what I say, and will not accept what I say.

That is OK – I get it, there are somethings in life we simply can not process, we can not deal with, so we go into fight or flight mode. Humans at times can do a very good impression of an Ostrich - bury head in sand and stick butt in the air.

As children we have a really simple brief – love and nurture and protect us. Sadly, for most of us, that doesn't happen and that can be because our parents did not have that or were not taught that themselves as children. So now we are in the situation where we are almost the opposite – we over love, we over nurture and we over protect our children. Creating a society that can not and does not know how to cope with life and the situations it presents us with.

So, each generation, has its own demons and its own issues that need to be addressed and remedied.

That my friends is a WHOLE other book on Ancestorial Karma / cleansing and why we are here. It can be a very Metaphysical and deep conversation to have.

SOOOOO – for me no legal action, no publicly naming and shaming my abusers, no publicly naming myself.

You may ask yourself right now – and rightly so. SO, what the hell is the purpose of all this then.

WELL – just because I like my privacy, just because I do not like the limelight, just because I choose my own path – does not mitigate what happened to me and how I feel about helping others. WHY do I need to be out there and in your face in the media or all over social media to make my case????

Why do you need to see me or know me to make my case?

Fact is – you do not.

You can read my words and you can see, hear or feel that you resonate with them or you do not. That is YOUR story.

I am here to tell you mine.

This Is MY TRUTH.

This DID happen.

This is HOW I dealt with it.

Sometimes the biggest problem you face in telling your story is the fact that people will simply brush you off as

- Oh another sexual abuse survivor – goodie
- Oh yep someone else who's family member hurt them as a child
- Oh here we go another women crying abuse
- Oh she is just jumping on the "me too" movement
- And on and on it goes.

So you do need to have a thick skin, you do need to have a really good support base around you.

Most important of all – believe in yourself.!

That is a tough one I know. We are very good (abuse survivors) of faking it till we make it. Showing the world the image, we want them to see. Pretending everything is just FINE.

Your voice. Your story.

This is not about anyone
else right now.

FINE yep one of my favourites and as discussed elsewhere – we all know what FINE is.

F(*&*&up

Insecure

Neurotic

Emotional

OMG I can not count the amount of times I said or yelled to my husband when I was going through therapy, when he asked how I was.

I AM F_I_N_E........ gosh I laugh now, because I really was just that – FINE. = Fucked up. Insecure. Neurotic and emotional = ALL THE TIME.

So, yet again I say what I have been saying right through this book so far.

You decide!

You do what works for you.

That is your empowerment, remember part of the journey back from abuse is regaining YOUR POWER.

Your voice. Your story.

This is not about anyone else right now.

CHAPTER TEN

Standing Strong and Being Who I Was Meant to Be

One day and maybe it is a long way in front of you yet, or a few days, weeks, month away....yet one day soon you will look back at your journey and be grateful for how far you have come.

To look back over all the things you have gone through and be grateful.

To be grateful for all these things in your life, the good, the bad and the ugly is truly EMPOWERING.

It is freeing and empowering and that AHA moment when you understand that everything in life happens for a reason.

Everything happens in divine timing. That is all huge news.

It is also that moment when you start living your life – your way, for you and being truly 100% yourself.

Nothing to prove to anyone else.

No one you need to impress but yourself.

Nothing you need to do but be yourself, who you were always meant to be and what you were always meant to be.

Living your life, your way for you and you alone.

That does not mean you have to be alone or live alone, but it means you live your life your way. You choose.

You will still have things that pop up now and again, you will still have things that trigger you.

What is different now is that you have the ability and tools to see things for what they really are, and deal with them.

One day and maybe it is a long way in front of you yet, or a few days, weeks, month away....yet one day soon you will look back at your journey and be grateful for how far you have come.

What I find now, is that I see things a lot sooner than I use to – for myself.

I also now have the tools and skills to overcome most of these things alone.

OR seek help if needed from a professional.

Am I perfect, far from it. Yet I also now know that I am not meant to be, none of us are. We are imperfectly perfect.

We are all unique and individual and our own person. Empowerment enables us to be comfortable in that skin, being our own unique selves.

I believe that we are always looking to grow and improve ourselves each and every day.

There is that old saying, "you learn something new each day". That is even truer about us. We keep learning about our strengths and weaknesses.

For your last thing to do in this book.

I want you to do a little self-check in.

Go through this list below and answer truthfully where you are right now.

It is a handy thing to keep as a PDF file somewhere and do a self-check in once a year.

1. What do you see as your greatest asset
2. What do you see as your biggest weakness
3. What do others see as your greatest asset, ask your family & friends here.
4. What do others see as your biggest weakness, ask your family & friends.
5. Look back over your life and create a timeline of events and things you have dealt with in your life so far.
6. What is your biggest regret in your life so far.
7. What area of your life do you wish to work on the most.
8. DO an inventory of your family and friends and list who you might need to move out of your life.
9. List why you feel you need to move these people out of your life.
10. What is your next goal in your life and how can you go about achieving this.

No one else will see this list or the results so feel free to be very open and honest with yourself here.

Keep the results handy as they are interesting to look back on over the coming years to see how far you have come on your journey.

Self-reflection is empowering in its simplicity. It takes no other tools than yourself and a notepad / computer.